Transfiguration

Poems by Mark Petterson

Kansas City Spartan Press Missouri

Spartan Press
Kansas City, Missouri
spartanpresskc.com

Copyright © Mark Petterson, 2019
First Edition1 3 5 7 9 10 8 6 4 2
ISBN: 978-1-950380-60-2
LCCN: 2019949454

Design, edits and layout: Jason Ryberg
Cover image: Jon Lee Grafton
Title page image: Mark Petterson
Author photo: Marie-Caroline Moir
All rights reserved. No part of this publication may be reproduced or transmitted in any form or by any means, electronic or mechanical, including photocopying, recording or by info retrieval system, without prior written permission from the author.

Acknowledgments:

Many thanks to the journals where these poems first appeared, in early or final forms:

"Ways of Survival" and "Forgiveness" - *CHARGE Magazine*
"Digging In" and "So Many Wrong Turns"- *Sun Star Review*
"Wedding at Cana" - *Freshwater Review*
"The Rainy Part of the World" - *Vending Machine Press*
"Contracts" and "Civil Procedure" - *Mojave River Review*
"Market" - *Stone Highway Review*
"Transfiguration" - *Blue Island Review*
"There are Times" - *The Mochila Review*

Special thanks to Laura Lucas, who was willing to read anything and everything I sent her, and never once betrayed any doubt about my work (even when she probably should have). Thanks to the Seattle crew: Phebe, Helena, Stephanie, Jonny, Katie, the women of WCCW, the Tent City 3 Writer's Group, and especially Rebecca Brown. My writing has had no greater friend than you.

Thanks to Mary Miller, who read many drafts of this book, and was ever-encouraging. Thanks to the faculty at Kansas and my MFA cohort, who slogged through my clumsy attempts at fiction and later, early iterations of this proect. To Jason Ryberg at Spartan Press for his editorial vision and dedication to making this book a reality.

Glen Butterworth, S.J., and Sr. Betty Daugherty, FSPA, who keep me grounded and motivated to pursue the cosmic Christ through art. Thanks to Iowa friends, especially Ethan and Nicole, for showing me what a lived commitment to justice means.

And to my mom, Karen, who instilled in me a love of reading and writing since as far back as I can remember, and has always been my most loyal support. Love you, mum.

TABLE OF CONTENTS

The Rainy Part of the World

The Rainy Part of the World / 1
Sound / 6
So Many Wrong Turns / 7
There Are Times / 8
Ways of Survival / 9
Forgiveness / 10

Other Gospels

Wedding at Cana / 15
Exorcism / 18
Walking on Water / 21
Transfiguration / 23
Lazarus / 25
Calming the Storm / 27
Fig Tree / 30
What We Do (in three parts) / 31
   (Short and Long) / 33
   (Ashes to Sparrows) / 34
Forgiving / 35
The Servant's Ear / 36
Resurrection / 37
St. James Looks Back at the End of His Life / 39

Detours

Contracts / 45

Civil Procedure / 49

Market / 51

Hiking / 53

Returning / 54

Research and Writing / 57

Beginning

Autumn, Cal Anderson Park / 61

Digging In / 63

Trail / 67

Bridges / 70

What It Is and What I Imagine It to Be / 73

Last, Happy / 74

*I also am other than what I imagine myself to be.
To know this is forgiveness.*

> ~ Simone Weil, "Void and Compensation,"
> *Gravity and Grace* (Routledge, translated by
> Crawford and von der Ruhr)

The Rainy Part of the World

The Rainy Part of the World

After the rundown middle school
where I tutor a thirteen-year-old who reads
at a second-grade level, and really we just read
comic books and he pretends he
is asleep and I feel helpless
though showing up is half the job,
to which I say, what is the other half?

I buy beer, come home,
plan on drinking off and on
throughout the night. I also
buy a pizza that proclaims on the
box, *Feasts for One!* and is
proud to be microwaveable –
as if us Ones are so busy and
have somewhere better to be, we
can only spare a minute to
cook a pizza, a Feast – and I put it
in the oven, because I think it might taste
better that way. Though you would
have told me that the oven just heats up
the house and we can't afford that.

*

I remember:
Moving in can taste like sour honey.
An extra curtain in the bathroom closet,
dirt in corners and under cushions
mixed with pieces of broken plastic.
Pimiento stains and cocktail
rings, visions of past losses,

waiting for release not coming.
The vapors coming off the radiator in the bedroom
have the smell of late autumn in Oxford.
There was a cat here once. I break
out in hives. The bits of paper and wine stains
around the breakfast nook is a lesson
on how to lose her.

When we saw this place first, and the
landlady squared us in the eye and asked us
if we were married, I pointed out
that the lease said nothing about the
relationship of cohabitants, or family
size or commitment to each other.
I wondered why she bothered. Was it
something about the clouds, so

far away, reflected into the kitchen
and the shadows on our faces?
You suggested that we brave the
coming thunder to go buy gin.
Gin sounded good to you on every
afternoon that it rained hot
rain.

*

Tragedy is everywhere, you said.
It's not something to be anxious about.
Lightning storm over the San Juans.
Waterspouts absorbing a fishing fleet.
Trip over a cat, down some stairs
and land on concrete. Simple.

You told me this at our first home,
as we watched a house floating down the interstate,
backing up what little traffic there was.
Nearly every low-lying field and yard underwater.
New lakes on roads near rivers where a levy breached

somewhere upstream.
And thank god that we only had this little apartment
on the third floor. I confessed my sin of complaining about
    the furniture
when we were moving in. The couches were so heavy. And
    Christ,
we had to use a pulley system to get your mother's
roll-top desk up to the bedroom.

All this only a month after the honeymoon. But it was nice
to walk around in the rain, both of us
under the umbrella, explore a brand new world of
islands and long-disused fishing boats

as we splashed around
in puddles and flung water with our hair.

And that thing with the tap water: I didn't mind so much.
You said: We won't take as many showers.
We'll wear clothes we haven't worn
in years. Eat off of paper plates,
and like we've always
wanted to do anyway, drink only beer
and wine with each other.

Sound

Fuck you, I said to the cat, who was blinking its knowing blink.
~ Ben Lerner, Leaving the Atocha Station

When we were younger, my brother and I,
we had this idea
that our language wasn't adequate
for mutual disappointments,
though we shared many of them,
so we reconstructed these things into
asking about the sound or the
mountain, and how much the fog
concealed one, or both, that day.

My brother, he said that it was impossible to
look at both at the same time, so it was nice
to think that one was clear while the other might
be obscured. You could always make out one,
the water or the rock, though it was never a straight shot,
Olympics to Rainier and points south.

After we had tried these metaphors, cobbled
from our limited capacities, we almost always
realized that maybe it was the best time
to make our way, less-than-sober, to the beach at
Alki, drive some flat-eyed rocks into the rippling
water, past the gulls, and wonder how we hadn't
thought of it before.

So Many Wrong Turns

> *Overheard*
> *Tully's Coffee*
> *Capitol Hill, Seattle*

Hey buddy
        Hey you
Seattle's gonna crash – Crack in half,
like an Easter egg - the big one's coming.

I'm no evangelist, just a concerned citizen.
        Just a person in-the-know.
The freeways will splinter.
The skyscrapers melt into jelly.

When? Soon.
        Tomorrow.
Why? Because.
History. Iniquity. So many wrong turns.

I'm on my way out of town.
        Just as soon as I get this coffee.
Stuck around to tell you, buddy.
Stayed here just to let you know.

There Are Times

we speak of lovers
as flowered thornbushes
motions of hand-on-skin

but you are just a good-looking mess
a song sung on a street corner
lingerie from a secondhand store
clinging to bent wire
finding solace in thrift
looking for a lover
in an old world

there is something settling
about these ways
that spices the elements and pleasures of difficulty
we don't doubt moments anymore
not without sight

because there are
thirteen ways of looking at a woman
thirteen ways to lose your mind

as if we know what it's like in heaven
telling each other about each other

Ways of Survival

learn the names of tree diseases

hold your hunting dog at the end of life

don't ask don't get attached

I had a friend once who wrecked his coupe; brain-damaged; moved back in

list all the possible anatomies of extreme aloneness

close your eyes when you start to see white

talk with your eyes, fingertips and hips

grow out your beard. cut it. keep it in your glove compartment

dry your eyes because the stone is rolled away

relax and look at maps of the world

Forgiveness

Be slow.
Read widely, without intent.
Give yourself no egress.

Be gentle,
touch without seeing.
Ask before you answer.

Be not afraid
of mourning, sadness, and even anger.
These are all real.
But do not be afraid.

The world is not about to cease -
it is not a sentence we can refuse to finish.
The stubborn showing of life beneath oppression
will neither cease nor flourish.

Wonder whether we all lose in the end.
And if it is possible to lose with love,
while still imagining
that this is not a game.

Not a fight, this invented splendor,
not an exercise for the clever.

Beyond anxiety, minutiae,
tedium, this is, after all, a lot of fun.

And though you wouldn't
have volunteered for it,
you will be right there,
right beside the rest of us.

Other Gospels

Wedding at Cana

John was giddy, looking for
eligible girls overcome with emotion
and no taste in men. All running here and
there, pouring drinks, cracking jokes

around Peter who, being married himself,
drank himself into a stupor.

Which might be why they ran
out of wine so quick, and all the
guests still there – they hadn't even
cut the cake.

*

I was sitting in the corner
making balloon animals for the kids,
so I saw the whole thing.

The bride's mother, hysterical,
was badgering the headwaiter – a man
of little faith but very practical
and desperate

who sent Mary
to see if her miracle-making
celebrity son
could do anything
about it.

*

Jesus just shook his head at her, then
waved the flat of his hand
and sent the wait
to go try the wash-water.

What they said about that stuff later
was true – better than most wedding
wine, and even John had to admit
that a cup of that red
was worth the whole trip down.

Exorcism

The day we stopped at the tombs,
I thought I might stop and pick up
some graveyard dirt, because you
never know when you might need
to fall in love, or win the lottery.
But the Master had different ideas.

He sought out the madman who lived
in the olive groves near the shoals
and told the crowd to gather around.
Some came, some stayed.

*

I've always thought that everyone
has demons in them, it's just that
some are more violent than others, and
maybe they should have put him in
an asylum, who knows? But

maybe he deserved the wild
like we deserved our seaside cottages
and pasty-eyed children.

John got upset, said out loud that
we were wasting out time – he was only
a demoniac. Only women found him
frightening.
Peter was frightened, too, and stayed
a safe distance behind our rabbi.

*

and language is a funny thing, because
the words that came out of his mouth while
Jesus was doing his thing, raising his hands
and proclaiming, those were not words,
but they made John weep as if they were
the saddest story in the world.

I tell you this because you have probably
heard from the pig farmers that the Master
is a bad man, that he does not care about
economic conditions. But I wanted you to know
that when I saw John cry like that,
I did not care about the fate of those
pigs very much at all.

Walking on Water

you might have heard about
that trick Christ pulled on us
out at the lake, the one where
he came running out over the waves

during the storm. John
Peter and I there, and how Peter
gripped the railing hard and
went over himself, even though

he had such a reputation
as a coward. and how no one
died. some kids saw the whole thing
I guess, now the whole damn neighborhood

has heard. you might have thought
we were big shots after that. celebrities.
and I guess we were, with the kids at least.
and the old women, because we knew him.

but when you live next to a lake
at the base of a mountain
it's harder to think of yourself as
so important after all.

and since I have heard that
most miracles have natural
explanations, I went yesterday
back to the middle of the lake

reached under boat and
there were rocks there
just under the surface
must have been growing for years.

so it turns out that
walking on water
wasn't built in a day
and miracles have beginnings.

Transfiguration

Stay there, he said,
and strode a few yards in front,
putting his hand up, flat, like
he was waiting for rain.

We were all out of our minds,
breathing like run horses
and doubled over,
having practically run up the mountain.

And that's when it occurred
though we all remember it
in different ways.

John's mouth dropped and
Peter, being the worst of us
and thus the most reverent,
fell face down and wept.
He had always been so fragile.

*

I, on the other hand, saw our friend
up there like a dancer with those two elderly,
glowing men, all fiery and exposed
to the wind and rain and I didn't want their fire
to go out or anything, since that would be
a shame, and I'm a practical man,
so after I got myself together I offered
to gather some sticks and palm leaves
and build a couple of shelters.

Christ, he just looked at me like I was an idiot,
with his hurricane eyes, since I suppose after all
none of them had a home down there
and why then should they want or need
one up here, closer to heaven?
He looked right at me, and through me,
and I felt ashamed, and so I just shut up
and stared for a few more hours
until he said it was time to go down.

Lazarus

he was not such a good man, not enough
at least to warrant resurrection.

I'd met him a couple of times - said a few
words, never impressed, went his own way.

John agreed, Peter was just sad as he
was whenever anything died, even a dog

so I guessed it was the grieving of the
women, their pleas and wails and tearing of hair

that convinced Him to do something, or
perhaps a sense of guilt as well

because he didn't get there in time,
preaching too long at Bethany, boring the peasants.

all this made me think that he was
more human than God, sometimes.

these eruptions of emotions, outbursts we
didn't see coming, unnecessary miracles, poor judgment

and I know that this caused some people
to fall away, and maybe that was his plan

but I tell you this just made me like him
even more, because he was one of us, and

if you saw those women smile like I did
you couldn't but help it to think it was alright.

Calming the Storm
After Rembrandt's "The Storm on the Sea of Galilee"

The evening began -
smelling like rotting seaweed,
salted winds, and bad decisions.
It had been such a long day –
parables spoken and explanations
left unsaid; deaf and confused
idiot disciples just trying to keep up
with what he had said yesterday.

I guess it would have taken
the wind out of anyone, because
though he never had a reputation
for being a deep sleeper,
he was dead snoring now.

*

Peter had already decided
that we were going to die,
clinging to the side of the boat
and puking up his portion
of the loaves and fishes.

John vainly tried to pull in
that rag of a sail, and I, in
a moment of madness,

crawled over to where Jesus
was sleeping
and pulled the pillow
from under his head.

The master opened one eye
pointed his index finger at the sky
and mouthed *calm*
the fuck down.

*

Later he gave us one of his
private sermons, never
recorded, noncanonical.

He told us: hindsight is so full of shit.
It waffles and turns and
leaves us with half-answers for things
that seemed important at the time:
to try and understand what just
happened.

Foresight is a kind grandparent. But she is rare,
and only comes to visit at cousins' weddings
and for funerals.

Pray for your desire because
god is in those,
and also in the place of our most hideous and
paralyzing fears.

*

And what I thought he was saying, is
that there is no place
we could go, where the light
and the shadow did not also go.
In desolation
storm
shame
and desire.

Fig Tree

that thing just fucking withered
like it was made
for nothing else on earth

What We Do

(in three parts)

you would think that maybe
we would sit around all
day discussing revolution -
the kingdom of god and all that,

and to be sure, Jesus had a lot to say
about the new order of things
and we wanted to know where
to find the cache of weapons
for the army of our rebellion.

but these were in the early days.
Peter liked to use the analogy of the weather,
storms and who knows where they come from,
while John made sure we all knew what
the term *collateral damage* meant.

but since then we didn't really know what he
was talking about, and maybe he didn't either.

we passed the time in other ways, too,
let the ideas circulate and settle,
see the people come and go, have some wine

his father Joseph, after a few too many
drinks, would tell us stories
about Jesus, when he was a child,
and we would listen like it
was the history of God himself.

(Short and Long)

so one time this certain rich fellow said to me:
'sir, make me a bed serviceable and comely.'
but I was sore troubled because the beam
he had given me was much too short.
Jesus was hanging around, like usual, and
said something to me, very softly: 'be not troubled,
but take hold of this beam by the one end
and I will by the other, and let us draw it out.'
and so, well, I did, and it worked. it just worked.
serviceable enough, at least, for that bed which
the rich man wanted.
so Jesus didn't say anything after that, just smiled
and I mumbled a thanks that I had such a son.

(Ashes to Sparrows)

*one afternoon, when he was about
eight years old, he took the clay that
came of some pool and made twelve miniature
sparrows. did I mention it was the Sabbath day
when Jesus did this? and the children of the Hebrews
came and said to me: 'lo, thy son was playing with us
and he took clay and made sparrows which
it was not right to do upon the Sabbath,
and he hath broken it.' and so of course,
being scared they might bully him, I went to
Jesus, and said to him: 'why are you doing
what is not right to do on the Sabbath?'
but Jesus said nothing and spread out his hands
and commanded the sparrows, saying:
'go forth into the height and fly:
ye shall not meet death at any man's hands.'
and they flew and began to cry out and praise God.
I let him do pretty much whatever he
wanted to do on the Sabbath after that.*

Forgiving

John was so angry during the whole
thing, didn't understand why He
was talking about sin and stone when
anyone with normal morals could see
that the woman was just plain guilty.
It got worse when Jesus ignored
his complaints, just kept sitting
in the wet sand and drawing shapes
with his fingertips.
Peter tried to blend in with the small crowd.
After a half-hour of silence, cut sometimes
by the sobbing of the woman, a few
lone jeers from old men, the crowd
began to drift away; bored with forgiveness,
going forth to sin a little more,
a little less, much the same maybe.
And I thought that maybe I recognized
the woman from a long time ago,
when I was a child, and the poor would
come to glean the leftovers from
my father's wheat, a long time ago.

The Servant's Ear

by that time most of us
understood that Christ wasn't
so hellbent on war as we had thought,
harbored few thoughts of revolution,
didn't see the point in challenging
Rome, but still, we wondered
maybe he wasn't so meek as to
let us all be arrested without
at least resisting or protest.
It was all three of us
who went for the sword, and
dumb luck that Peter was closest,
swung blind, clipped the side
of the boy's face and not knowing
what we had done, stepped back
to see if we would get
what was coming to us.

Resurrection

so then, a lot of people
around here
believers, at least, said
that his last miracle was
rising from the dead

which was impressive of
course, and symbolic,
the garden earthquake and
angels all around the women
because, I mean, who
does that?

or maybe the ascension
all with it the power and
the glory
that we now associate with
him rising and clouding
like we see in paintings
and visions and in dreams

but the other day
I ran into an old friend
of mine at a Samarian tavern
who told me, over many beers

that he had seen Jesus
on the road to Emmaus.
just appeared, walking,
asking questions like a visitor

at the house, invited himself in,
had some bread, blessed it,
as if only he could do that.

St. James Looks Back at the End of His Life

I am an old man now
and tend towards thinking
back in time, not forward,
like in our youth. Past lovers,
friends, a little, yes.
But mostly I think of
those three years with
the Master, the great flaring
forth of our movement —
whether it was all a dream
or we had just made it all up.

I re-read sometimes
the letters I wrote
to the brand-new churches,
garbage mostly, springtime
hopefulness and the harsh
rebukes of a terrified father,
sensing danger in and around
every corner and in every dark
place, monsters who might devour
his firstborn.

*

I am not quite sure what to make
of the accounts my friends have written
about Jesus. They seem larger-than-life,
the miracles getting marquee billing
and, to be honest, there is a lot
of unnecessary editorializing as to
his nature. We were always uncomfortable
with mystery.

You can read those for yourself.
Create your own conclusions.
But this morning, after strolling
up the little mountain outside of town
which is my habit in the morning,
and watching the Iberian merchants
scramble around the square, like
pebbles blown in wandering eddies,
I could not remember a single miracle,
nor one parable. It is a feeling I have grown
accustomed to, as I sometimes do not
remember the names of my own children,
or where they live now.

*

Between the gusts of wind through
the olive trees and the whistling
of goatherds wandering with
their wards up and down the winding path
up the mountain, my mind was
able to latch onto one thing he said,
probably because he said it to us
more than he said anything else.
Don't be afraid.

He said this more than he
talked about the Father,
more than he rambled about his mission,
even more than his obsessive
arguments with the Pharisees.
And true, we were a fearful bunch.
But I didn't understand it
at the time, why he repeated himself
so often.

We misunderstood, I think.
We always took it as an admonishment
about the present situation,
whatever that might have been –
demons, drowning, leprosy.
But now that I am older
I think he might have been
trying to tell us
that there are other ways to be,
and other worlds are possible.

*

I am better with mystery now,
though I am in no shape
to do anything about it
nor have the desire to share
this revelation with any young ones.
I think I will stay on this hill as long as
I can, perhaps fall asleep for a while,
and remember what I can while I dream.

Detours

Contracts

a few times, to a mason jar
filled with rosemary and gin
I have wondered whether
those noises down the alley
are the hammering of iron and
aluminum

gates and nails and maybe
a scarecrow into the backstreet
neighbor's garden sill.
or if they are instead reports
from a small boy's
gun

and then whether it is
his toy, or his father's toy,
or am I just hearing things
sitting on the back stoop,
waiting for you.

*

we make these promises
to ourselves. to the sawgrass,
to the ranges. maybe things
will get better, or tomorrow
we'll just be left, holding the
last echo.

and the neighbors say the neighborhood
is going to the birds and I say I
don't know what that means
because I see birds here and there
but do you have more to drink?

*

it's easier this way,
in an economy of remedies,
waiting for gyres off-balance
and young. And you. You
there with violence and peonies,
accusing me of just gathering material,
not really interested.

it's just a design defect, I said,
not market tested, loose things.
A calculus of public insurance
gone bad.

*

Take the cactus and go. I've killed
it anyway. It was an accident.
I poured day-old beer into the
cactus mug every few days.
And beer is mostly water but maybe
it just grew too much
and felt constrained,
died of a broken heart.

An accident, like I said.
Equally persuaded that it
all comes down to something like
ordinariness. Workable for some
and too-heavy for others.

Civil Procedure

We have become specialists
at conflict.

Like in that story you read to me
before you hid it under the fire,
where the wife throws a glass of red
wine at the protagonist because he
bought a motorcycle, without telling her,
and it leaves a stain on the white
wallpaper, in the shape of a man,
hiding his face in his
upended palms.

We should have made some rules.
Compiled some casebook that would have
helped in these futures with others.

As if we couldn't find the point
the issue the gist the tip of my tongue
to reserve summary judgment
and we should have made some rules.

Like: no stories to convey meanings.
Like: no throwing wine like in that story.
Maybe: don't contradict yourself.

This kind of user manual, you could
really make a killing selling it. Give
specific warnings about us, and what sort
of things we're apt to get into when I think
we might be headed into a logical corner,
of our own special design.
If you included a few mistakes, gave flawed
advice, you could keep the customers
coming until they've forgotten who I
was entirely.

And then the novelty factor, too.
It would sell itself – look at this sad
sack misery addict. So very funny.

But anyway, I think I am going to keep
the motorcycle.

Market

these are things to be serious about.

frozen fresh canned in oil or water
breast meat drumsticks or some sort of fish
instead. and how lean is lean enough?
which sort of spice was it? cumin or ground
cinnamon did you say to get? how much, brand name?
and I wonder what percent live culture is best
in the raspberry yogurt

while I pass by the powdered milk, and try
to calculate where what might have been,
I imagine I've heard somewhere that
avocados are bad for the liver
(or was it the other way around) and
never buy iceberg heads — that was
you. I can't keep it straight

because all the while in the bright lights
I am drawn by a gravity
towards the frozen pizza, the same way
you talk about ice cream (and pickles
when you were pregnant) although you never
bought that rocky road

I do the shopping now

what about this pita that comes with
free hummus? am I getting taken?
only local honey, you said, I said I know
that, almond milk but no nuts in the
cereal. and did the doctor say
that french fries were alright?

watch out for my baby
a woman says as I turn the corner,
my cart facing diapers and soda,
but she is somewhere down the
aisle, not speaking to me
not looking for me

so I give up with what I've got
check out, walk out, rain, think,
this is so much

Hiking

From Ambleside
I should have known better
Than to choose a trail called
The Struggle.

Returning

First, imagine the customer service desk.
Trickles of unhappy people
— capitalism being the great leveler —
all of us equal in a consuming misery,

toting plastic sundries large
and small.
Coffeemakers televisions
rolls of painter's tape underwear
a green kid's bicycle.

Listen:
this didn't work right.
doesn't fit me.
i broke it.

And the most common:
it was a gift.
This excuse is always accepted
as valid, for as bad as it can
get behind the counter at
the department of misery,

where even the most
stoney of souls
knows how it is like
to receive a thing,

unwanted, unloved, given
by a friend or relative,
however well-meaning,
who only wanted

to make you happy with
that box of puzzle pieces
or candles or sweater or
toaster.

But it doesn't make you happy.
You hate it, in fact.
You smile, and say,
bless your heart and yet
hold a black hate, a contempt,
in your heart because
this person should know,
should understand
what you want,
what brings you joy,
and yet doesn't.

And you are ashamed at the same time.

But you don't need to be.
It's a choice. You are returning.

We are always returning. It is a re-opening
of choices made, both an assertion
of control over things you never thought
were yours to decide. And also
an acceptance of things that
were not and are not yours
to control.

So take it back. Don't tell your
sister or aunt or child that you
returned their gift. Make yourself
happy. Apologize to the comrade at
customer service; say that we've all
been there, and that's shitty.
Then go home.

Just like a poem is never finished.
You are always co-creating meaning.

You don't even need to know that it is happening.

Research and Writing

I have a complaint. Let me spell it out.

I asked you to hold onto something for me.
And keep it simple keep it sheltered.

You said it's hard to keep
a handful of dust, a fistful of rain.

If it were easy, if silence could be
deemed acceptance, then we could find

there's been some movement here,
says the last one who stayed.
Letters across the ocean, phone calls from
the sky.

Ask, is my suffering worth less now
because I have had more, because
it is a pattern?

Then finally, let's end.
So give us a cheer
give us the old college try
give us Barabbas
and give us a prayer.

Beginning

Autumn, Cal Anderson Park

Once again, in the park,
drifting off, imagining the recurring
exchange – I try to explain to you the
plot and turn of the book
I've been reading for almost
all of our relationship.

What seems like forever.
On the same bench, too, across
the path from a bronze plaque
about the Great Seattle Fire
of 1889. The city fathers built
this park immediately after the fire,
though it did not open until
twelve years later, for reasons
that are still unclear.

No one who has read this story, I say,
in this fiction of a conversation,
can remember who the protagonist
was, or forget for what it was
that he or she was revered.

In the same way, so strong
was the impression
in that story, that the shape
of a shattering wine glass

and the outline of the stain
on the shadowed sidewalk
become indelible, inky and pale.

Cal Anderson won two bronze
stars, two commendation medals.
Died young of AIDS. *We are not
monsters* he said, a week
after his equal rights bill died
for the seventeenth straight year
on the floor of the Washington
state legislature.

The sound of a Buick turning
over makes me start. I see
birds arguing over
spilled kettle corn
and a shadow of what
looked for a brief moment
like your blue umbrella.

Fourteen years after his death,
a magazine named the park as
one of the best parks in America.
It sure seems so in autumn,
winding along the wine-stained
sidewalks. So positioned,
halfway transformed. Plotting
an outline of the main points
of a story on a sea of meandering
paths.

Digging In

> *I'll dig in, into my days, having come here to live, not to visit.*
> ~ Denise Levertov, *Settling*

Sunday morning, raccoons outside the window, at it again.
 I was reading Levertov's *Evening Train* and waiting for
the coffee to kick in.

Audible shuffling surrounded by screeches and maybe the
 cries of a toddler who has lost a toy or a cat who has lost
a limb.

Took out my phone. Shazaam-ed the noises. Googled rats
 and cats and pigeons.

Nothing doing, read some interesting things before I saw what
 was actually going on. Two raccoons out there, screwing
like there was no tomorrow.

In a tree. Just above my window.

Staring at me the whole time. Like a couple of goddamn lunatics.

I read, on Wikipedia, that raccoon life is pretty much entirely
 composed of three activities – rummaging through the
garbage, scurrying under the neighbor's porch, and fucking.

Though raccoons are extremely intelligent, these behaviors that compose the primary canon are mostly instinctive, according to biologists and, to me at least, acceptable activities for wild animals.

The problem happens when humans get involved.

For example: a friend kept a raccoon as a sort of outdoor pet for a few months, leaving out dry cat food behind his garage and keeping his cat indoors. Eventually the cat escaped through an open window and challenged the raccoon. Friend broke up the fight while wearing oven mitts and a catcher's mask.

Another thing that Wikipedia told me was that raccoons remember specific tasks and sequences, like the numerical code to a padlock or the weekly route of a garbage truck. They can retain this information for up to three years, but usually only live two years, in the wild.

Also, one time I took a BuzzFeed quiz: *Is your boyfriend a good guy or just a raccoon?* After answering the last question that yes, indeed, he is often found scurrying under the neighbor's porch, BuzzFeed told me that my boyfriend was actually just a raccoon and they were sorry they had to tell me that.

I had recently moved into this apartment with a view of the mountain through the thin spires of a hanging willow. Moved to Seattle after heartbreaks plenty, to find a center of something again.

But I didn't really have a clear vision of what that might look like.
Maybe herons would appear and perch in a nearby tree, maybe the mountain would audibly speak its majesty, or the Sound would reveal its secrets and tranquility.

Raccoons appeared in the tree, the mountain was rarely ever visible in the fog, and all I heard about the Sound were stories of terrifying giant octopuses that were maybe or maybe not trying to escape the aquarium and, I assume, come to my apartment and eat me.

And that Sunday, it was the beginning of Lent.

Not a time, I know, to be preparing for mass by staring at a couple of raccoons engaging in their natural non-human animal act.

There's not quite an apt enough metaphor for the frustration that happens when you're trying to be spiritual somehow, to look at the mountain, to imagine majesty or something, and all you can hear is the ungodly screeching of two amorous street critters and imagine that they were sent by the devil himself to distract you and make you unholy or something.

The piety I was looking for never came that morning.
The peace, that transcendent moment, the *shanti* that I had come to the city looking for, never arrived.

Or at least I didn't notice it, as transfixed and driven to distraction as I was by the sights and sounds of my little neighbors who just wanted to have a good old raccoon time.

The mountain didn't sing a canticle of creation, the clouds didn't even break.

I made it to mass eventually, and while I spent most of the service in the back pew reading the Levertov poems that I had not been able to focus on that morning, I think even that can be a religious act.

The mountain was still there that evening. The raccoons were still there. They still hissed at me. The clouds were still there, unbroken, the mountain still stood silent, in its dumb witnessing presence.

Trail

In the afternoon I followed a weasel into the forest
and, indeed, a fly, by its constant buzzing
around, and sometimes in, my ear
forced me from a perch on the *meditation balcony*
and into one of the very unclear paths surrounding the lake
at the Trappist monastery.

The weasel just happened to be in front of me,
and turned a few times to stare, as if to say,
I see you, big guy, and to invite me along for the
journey. He took me along a lakeside trail
and I swatted at flies, feeling guilty for
trying to harm a living thing at a monastery,
of all places.

We crossed a few shaky footbridges around moss-encrusted
stone and cheery lush ivy that had
wrapped its way around every thing, living or dead.

We passed a street sign, hung on a tree:
Yankee Stadium, This Way.
We made a left turn, away from the lake
and I thought, does this trail know where it's
going? Should it be a trail that winds around the lake?
Why are we heading deeper into the woods, away from the lake?

I thought of what Joan, the lady who works at the monastery
bookstore and lives in the nearby village, had told me.
Better stick to the roads. The trunk road. Yes,
that's your best bet. Can't get lost on the trunk road. The monks
are getting old and don't keep up the trails very well anymore.
But I had ignored Joan's advice
and was now following a lakeside trail that was
no longer beside the lake.

The flies were gone, at least. I was moving fast enough.
The weasel and I were moving swiftly, into the woods,
and I was becoming more and more worried
because Sean, a seminarian who was doing a retreat
had told me that he, an almost-man-of-god
(or is it man-of-almost-god), had himself become lost
on the trails a few times that day. He had told me
this over dinner, and I had been surprised,
because I didn't know it was OK to talk
during dinner, since the Trappists are a silent
order, but whatever, I guess.

And anyway, as I was despairing and falling
deeper into regret over this choice to follow the weasel,
the trail made an abrupt u-turn, jutting back
to the lake and putting me within sight of
the guesthouse, where I was to sleep that night.
The weasel was gone by now, an imp back to
his forest playground, and I was on my way home.

As I crossed the last footbridge, I saw a sign
that someone had planted above the sawgrass
at the water's edge. *Walking on Water Prohibited.
Monks Only.*

Bridges
for RB

I have always been the one
who, like George Costanza,
swerves to avoid the pigeon
and runs over the squirrel.

Claims *we don't have a deal
with the squirrels!* to a
horrified soon-to-be-ex lover in the seat
next to me.

*

Who among us befriends
the smallest of pests?
What kind of a person
is that? And what does that
say about me?

Names them? Adopts them?
Develops concern for them.

A better person than I.
Someone in tune with vibrant matter,
with the thinglyness of all creation.

*

I thought of Longview, Washington:
they built bridges over roadways
for a million little rodents
would seem like a
waste of time; a cheap
nod to whimsy.

But *you've* seen the squirrels
after they cross.
Like Julian, you've
seen a vision in your
room five thousand miles away.
As the roof plaster crumbles off
Into the hand of supplicating pilgrims.

*

You hear their whispers
and they are grateful.

For you know their ways.
They gather in units, packs, clans, pods.

Light strike-anywhere matches as torches,
little furry druids
chanting for the good graces of the divine and
the wisdom of their ancestors.

They have a plan:
if fire, scurry.
If flood, tree.
And they are grateful for
this magic in the sky
built by some benevolent
unknowable god

The same one for whom you've been searching
for almost all of your life.

What It Is and What I Imagine It to Be

they are not the same

fair condition, you said
well, fair is better than poor
like me, and fair has some
positive connotations
like blonde, just, Victorian
pale with freckles. I can
imagine much worse, and
the more I think about it
the more I am looking forward
to seeing it.

some scratches, you said
but then, everyone has some
dings and nicks, don't they? no
one is perfect. these make
everything unique.
whitewashed tombs.

seen a lot of use, you said
that's great - means people
think they've got something
worthwhile. I think this
is going to turn out
all right.

Last, Happy

And so it is spring,
or at least what feels like
the itching and solace of southwest wind,
the first sips of bourbon water
on the secondhand couch
on my secondhand porch in the
shadow of the college lights.

The neighbors across the street, sophomores
all of them, are watching Missouri
get crushed, and laughing while they might as well.
I sometimes wish I were them.

*

But as it is, I am here, and
I am listening to some music you gave me
before we divorced for the second time.
You drove out of the fog, remember?
It was the car your mother bought us
filled with crockery and brand-new sheets,
the highest thread-count. And she was so happy
then, looking at her only daughter happy,
or smiling at least. Said she had waited for
so long.

I teach these kids, across the street,
every Tuesday and Thursday, and they
sit there and close their eyes when I talk
about modern poetry and its charms
if we'd just let it affect us. I like to think
that they are daydreaming.

The southwest wind in Kansas used to
whip and wave your hair and you would complain
but then you would tell your mother
that it was what you liked most about this place.

I've been out here for a while.

*

Thinking, for some reason,
as it becomes morning
that we might, without reason,
maybe next spring
be
at long last, happy

Mark Petterson earned his MFA in creative writing at the University of Kansas. He grew up in Prairie Village, Kansas, and now lives in Iowa City, where he teaches writing at the University of Iowa. This is his first collection of poetry.